PASS–ALONG
Promises

Inspiration for
FRIENDS

© 2005 by Barbour Publishing, Inc.

ISBN 1-59310-641-6

Scripture quotations are taken from the *Holy Bible,* New
Living Translation, copyright © 1996. Used by permis-
sion of Tyndale House Publishers, Inc. Wheaton,
Illinois 60189, U.S.A. All rights reserved.

Cover and interior images © Photonica

Published by Barbour Publishing, Inc., P.O. Box 719,
Uhrichsville, Ohio 44683, www.barbourbooks.com

*Our mission is to publish and distribute inspirational prod-
ucts offering exceptional value and biblical encouragement to
the masses.*

Member of the
Evangelical Christian
Publishers Association

Printed in China.
5 4 3 2

PASS-ALONG
Promises

Inspiration for
FRIENDS

WRITTEN AND COMPILED BY
HOPE CLARKE

BARBOUR
PUBLISHING

God does notice us,
and He watches over us.
But it is usually through
another person that
He meets our needs.

SPENCER W. KIMBALL

$\mathcal{T}$HE HEARTFELT COUNSEL OF A

FRIEND IS AS SWEET AS PERFUME

AND INCENSE.

PROVERBS 27:9

· ·

Love is an image of God,
and not a lifeless image,
but the living essence of
the divine nature
which beams full of
all goodness.

MARTIN LUTHER

· · ·

· ·

"AND HERE IS HOW TO MEASURE

IT—THE GREATEST LOVE IS SHOWN

WHEN PEOPLE LAY DOWN THEIR

LIVES FOR THEIR FRIENDS."

JOHN 15:13

· ·

You have made me
a better person by
encouraging me to be
the best that I can be.

· · · ·

· ·

$\mathcal{A}$s iron sharpens iron,

a friend sharpens a friend.

Proverbs 27:17

*My friends are
my estate.*

EMILY DICKINSON

. . .

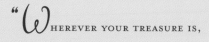

"**W**HEREVER YOUR TREASURE IS,

THERE YOUR HEART AND

THOUGHTS WILL ALSO BE."

MATTHEW 6:21

Your friendship is
an anchor in
a tumultuous world.

. . .

$\mathcal{A}$ FRIEND IS ALWAYS LOYAL.

PROVERBS 17:17

Thank you for loving me
and accepting me as I am.
. . .

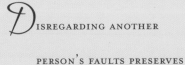

*D*ISREGARDING ANOTHER PERSON'S FAULTS PRESERVES LOVE; TELLING ABOUT THEM SEPARATES CLOSE FRIENDS.

PROVERBS 17:9

The better part of
one's life consists of
his friendships.

ABRAHAM LINCOLN

· · ·

REAL FRIEND STICKS CLOSER

THAN A BROTHER.

PROVERBS 18:24

*Friendship improves happiness
and abates misery by
doubling our joys
and dividing our grief.*

JOSEPH ADDISON

· · ·

$\mathcal{W}$HEN OTHERS ARE HAPPY, BE

HAPPY WITH THEM. IF THEY ARE

SAD, SHARE THEIR SORROW.

ROMANS 12:15

Your love is
a beacon of strength and truth.
It neither wavers
nor grows dim.

. . .

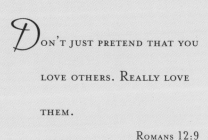

DON'T JUST PRETEND THAT YOU

LOVE OTHERS. REALLY LOVE

THEM.

ROMANS 12:9

You have
always believed in me. . . .
Thank you for
being my friend!

· · ·

*L*OVE EACH OTHER WITH GENUINE

AFFECTION, AND TAKE DELIGHT

IN HONORING EACH OTHER.

ROMANS 12:10

*Let us have faith
that right makes might.*

ABRAHAM LINCOLN

. . .

$\mathcal{N}$EVER PAY BACK EVIL FOR EVIL TO

ANYONE. DO THINGS IN SUCH A

WAY THAT EVERYONE CAN SEE

YOU ARE HONORABLE.

ROMANS 12:17

. . . .

I count myself
in nothing else so happy as
in a soul rememb'ring
my good friends.

WILLIAM SHAKESPEARE

. . .

. . . .

LIVE IN HARMONY WITH EACH

OTHER. DON'T TRY TO ACT

IMPORTANT, BUT ENJOY THE

COMPANY OF ORDINARY PEOPLE.

ROMANS 12:16

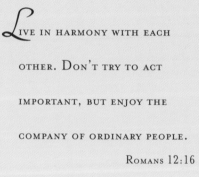

*You make me happy
just because you're you!*

$\mathcal{W}$E WERE FILLED WITH LAUGHTER,

AND WE SANG FOR JOY.

PSALM 126:2

· ·

You have
so many gifts
to offer the world.

· · ·

· ·

GOD HAS GIVEN EACH OF US THE

ABILITY TO DO CERTAIN THINGS

WELL. . . . IF YOUR GIFT IS THAT

OF SERVING OTHERS, SERVE THEM

WELL. . . . AND IF YOU HAVE A

GIFT FOR SHOWING KINDNESS TO

OTHERS, DO IT GLADLY.

ROMANS 12:6–8

No lapse of time
or distance of place
can lessen the friendship of
those who are truly persuaded
of each other's worth.

ANONYMOUS

$\mathcal{B}$E ENCOURAGED AND KNIT

TOGETHER BY STRONG TIES

OF LOVE.

COLOSSIANS 2:2

*A friend listens
with her heart.*

BONNIE JENSEN

· · ·

"GOD BLESSES THOSE WHOSE

HEARTS ARE PURE, FOR THEY

WILL SEE GOD."

MATTHEW 5:8

*I am inspired
and encouraged
by your beliefs.*

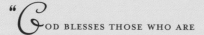

"GOD BLESSES THOSE WHO ARE

PERSECUTED BECAUSE THEY

LIVE FOR GOD, FOR THE

KINGDOM OF HEAVEN IS

THEIRS."

MATTHEW 5:10

Your gentleness of spirit
and kind words
soothe the troubled soul.

"GOD BLESSES THOSE WHO ARE

GENTLE. . .FOR THE WHOLE

EARTH WILL BELONG TO

THEM."

MATTHEW 5:5

I have learned that
to have a good friend is
the purest of all God's gifts,
for it is a love that has
no exchange of payment.

FRANCES FARMER

$\mathcal{L}$IVE A LIFE FILLED WITH LOVE

FOR OTHERS.

EPHESIANS 5:2

*Friendship is
a sheltering tree.*

SAMUEL TAYLOR COLERIDGE

. . .

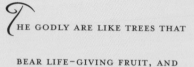

THE GODLY ARE LIKE TREES THAT

BEAR LIFE-GIVING FRUIT, AND

THOSE WHO SAVE LIVES ARE WISE.

PROVERBS 11:30

Your words. . .
your ways. . .
your thoughts
honor God by
their kindnesses.
. . .

$\mathcal{G}$ODLINESS HELPS PEOPLE ALL

THROUGH LIFE.

PROVERBS 13:6

*God knew
the seasons of life would bring
sunshine and rain. . .
for both He created
the shelter of friendship.*

BONNIE JENSEN

$\mathcal{W}$ISDOM IS ENSHRINED IN AN

UNDERSTANDING HEART.

PROVERBS 14:33

*You always know
just the right thing to say.*

. . .

$\mathcal{W}$ORDS SATISFY THE SOUL AS

FOOD SATISFIES THE STOMACH;

THE RIGHT WORDS ON A

PERSON'S LIPS BRING

SATISFACTION.

PROVERBS 18:20

A true friend unbosoms freely,
advises justly, assists readily,
adventures boldly,
takes all patiently,
defends courageously,
and continues
a friend unchangeably.

WILLIAM PENN

TWO PEOPLE CAN ACCOMPLISH MORE

THAN TWICE AS MUCH AS ONE;

THEY GET A BETTER RETURN

FOR THEIR LABOR. IF ONE

PERSON FALLS, THE OTHER CAN

REACH OUT AND HELP.

ECCLESIASTES 4:9–10

When I have
opened my heart to a friend,
I am more myself than ever.

THOMAS MOORE

. . .

WISDOM IS MORE PRECIOUS THAN

RUBIES; NOTHING YOU DESIRE

CAN COMPARE WITH HER. SHE

OFFERS YOU LIFE IN HER RIGHT

HAND, AND RICHES AND HONOR

IN HER LEFT.

PROVERBS 3:15–16

Your love encompasses
those who surround you.
It is a love
that knows no bounds.

. . .

$\mathcal{D}$EAR FRIENDS, LET US CONTINUE

TO LOVE ONE ANOTHER, FOR

LOVE COMES FROM GOD.

ANYONE WHO LOVES IS BORN

OF GOD AND KNOWS GOD.

1 JOHN 4:7

I know that
I can always depend on you.
(Know that you can
depend on me, too.)

. . .

GOD WILL SURELY DO THIS FOR

YOU, FOR HE ALWAYS DOES JUST

WHAT HE SAYS.

1 CORINTHIANS 1:9

Friends are
life's little
"pick-me-uppers."

BONNIE JENSEN

· · ·

$\mathcal{F}$OLLOW ONLY WHAT IS GOOD.

REMEMBER THAT THOSE WHO DO

GOOD PROVE THAT THEY ARE

GOD'S CHILDREN.

3 JOHN 1:11

From the day we met,
I knew you would be
my friend forever.

. . .

After David had finished talking with Saul, he met Jonathan, the king's son. There was an immediate bond of love between them, and they became the best of friends.

1 Samuel 18:1

When I am
hurt or weary,
you bring me comfort.

. . .

*N*EVER ABANDON A FRIEND.

PROVERBS 27:10

Your words are
precious to me.

. . .

*G*ET THE TRUTH AND DON'T EVER

SELL IT; ALSO GET WISDOM,

DISCIPLINE, AND DISCERNMENT.

PROVERBS 23:23

Joy and meaning are
often found in
the simple things of life.

. . .

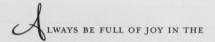

Always be full of joy in the

Lord. I say it again—

rejoice!

Philippians 4:4

Blessed is
the influence of one true,
loving human soul on another.

GEORGE ELIOT

. . .

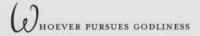

$\mathcal{W}$HOEVER PURSUES GODLINESS

AND UNFAILING LOVE WILL FIND

LIFE, GODLINESS, AND HONOR.

PROVERBS 21:21

. . . .

Your love for God is
reflected by the
shining mirror of your soul.

. . .

. . . .

" 'You must love the Lord your God with all your heart, all your soul, and all your mind.' This is the first and greatest commandment."

Matthew 22:37–38

True prayer is
not to be found in
the words of the mouth
but in the thoughts of
the heart.

GREGORY THE GREAT

. . .

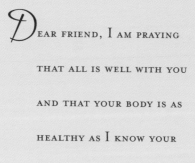

*D*EAR FRIEND, I AM PRAYING

THAT ALL IS WELL WITH YOU

AND THAT YOUR BODY IS AS

HEALTHY AS I KNOW YOUR

SOUL IS.

3 JOHN 1:2

I laugh the most when
I laugh with you.
. . .

*S*o rejoice in the Lord and be

glad, all you who obey him!

Shout for joy, all you whose

hearts are pure!

Psalm 32:11

*The heart that loves is
always young.*

GREEK PROVERB

. . .

𝒫RAISE THE LORD, FOR HE HAS

SHOWN ME HIS UNFAILING LOVE.

PSALM 31:21

In the presence of a friend,
may you find
true comfort and peace.

. . .

*T*HOSE WHO LOOK TO HIM FOR

HELP WILL BE RADIANT WITH JOY;

NO SHADOW OF SHAME WILL

DARKEN THEIR FACES.

PSALM 34:5

*I thank God for
all things good—
peace, happiness,
laughter, friends.*

BONNIE JENSEN

"*I* tell you, use your worldly resources to benefit others and make friends. In this way, your generosity stores up a reward for you in heaven."

LUKE 16:9

Lord of hopefulness,
Lord of all joy,
Whose trust, ever childlike,
no cares could destroy.
Be there at our waking,
and give us, we pray,
Your bliss in our hearts,
Lord, at the break of day.

FROM "ALL DAY HYMN," BY J. STRUTHER

"I HAVE TOLD YOU ALL THIS SO THAT YOU MAY HAVE PEACE IN ME. HERE ON EARTH YOU WILL HAVE MANY TRIALS AND SORROWS. BUT TAKE HEART, BECAUSE I HAVE OVERCOME THE WORLD."

JOHN 16:33

*Never shall I forget
the days I spent with you.
Continue to be my friend,
as you will always
find me yours.*

LUDWIG VAN BEETHOVEN

. . .

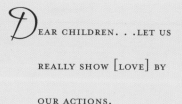

DEAR CHILDREN. . .LET US

REALLY SHOW [LOVE] BY

OUR ACTIONS.

1 JOHN 3:18

. . . .

*I admire your ability
to see the positive side
of every situation.*

. . .

. . . .

THE LORD IS KING! LET THE EARTH

REJOICE! LET THE FARTHEST

ISLANDS BE GLAD.

PSALM 97:1

*Your patience
and strength of character
have been an inspiration to me.*

. . .

CONSIDER THE FARMERS WHO EAGERLY

LOOK FOR THE RAINS IN THE FALL

AND IN THE SPRING. THEY PATIENTLY

WAIT FOR THE PRECIOUS HARVEST TO

RIPEN. YOU, TOO, MUST BE PATIENT.

AND TAKE COURAGE, FOR THE

COMING OF THE LORD IS NEAR.

JAMES 5:7–8